Fun Fabrics of the 50s

Joy Shih

Schiffer Publishing Ltd

77 Lower Valley Road, Atglen, PA 19310

Dedication

To my mother, Evelyn Shih, who trusted me with the family sewing machine
and my sister, Gloria, who willingly allowed me to create wierd stuff for her to wear

ISBN: 0-7643-0173-X

Published by Schiffer Publishing, Ltd.
77 Lower Valley Road
Atglen, PA 19310
Phone: (610) 593-1777
Fax: (610) 593-2002
Please write for a free catalog.
This book may be purchased from the publisher.
Please include $2.95 for shipping.
Try your bookstore first.

We are interested in hearing from authors
with book ideas on related subjects.

Library of Congress Cataloging-in-Publication Data

Shih, Joy.
    Fun fabrics of the 50s / Joy Shih.
        p.   cm.
    ISBN 0-7643-0173-X
    1. Textile fabrics--United States--History--20th
century--Themes, motives. I. Title.
NK8812.S55 1996
746'.0973'09045--dc20   96-25445
                                              CIP

Contents

Introduction

The 1950s was an interesting time in history. Americans happy to be "back home" after a world war were excited about new technology, fascinated with faster modes of transportation, impassioned with 'rockin' new music, and heavily into making babies. Fabric designs popular during this period reflect all those feelings and more.

The decade's designers commonly unified nature with technology, resulting in interesting mixtures of florals and geometric patterns. Newer and better dyes meant brighter colors, and bolder experimentation with color combinations. The post-war baby boom created a new industry in "juvenile" designs. Television westerns with its heroes started a "Wild West" craze. Circus-themed movies were represented by fanciful fabric designs featuring clowns and big-top animals. The advent of rock 'n' roll influenced the creation of a "teen culture" eager to experiment with adventurous new colors and unrestrained patterns. Domestic tranquility and the end of the war renewed interest in world travel, especially to "exotic" destinations such as Mexico, Hawaii, and Egypt. Returning servicemen brought back many romantic images of France and soon poodles, berets and artists' palettes became fashionable. In the home, fruits and vegetables splashed across kitchens in wild colors on curtains, tablecloths, and aprons.

The fun fabrics represented in these pages were found in leading department stores and dry goods retailers during the 1950s. You might recognize Dad's cotton plaid shirt, Grandma's "duster", Mom's apron, Suzy's pedal pushers, Bobby's "Daniel Boone" PJs, or even the smock worn by the clerk at Woolworth's. Enjoy!

Florals

13

14

17

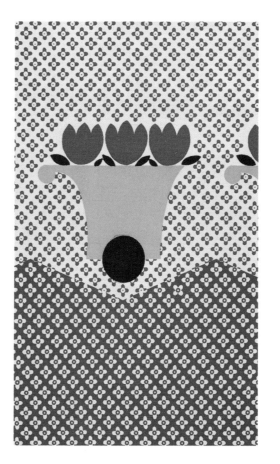

23

24

25

28

33

34

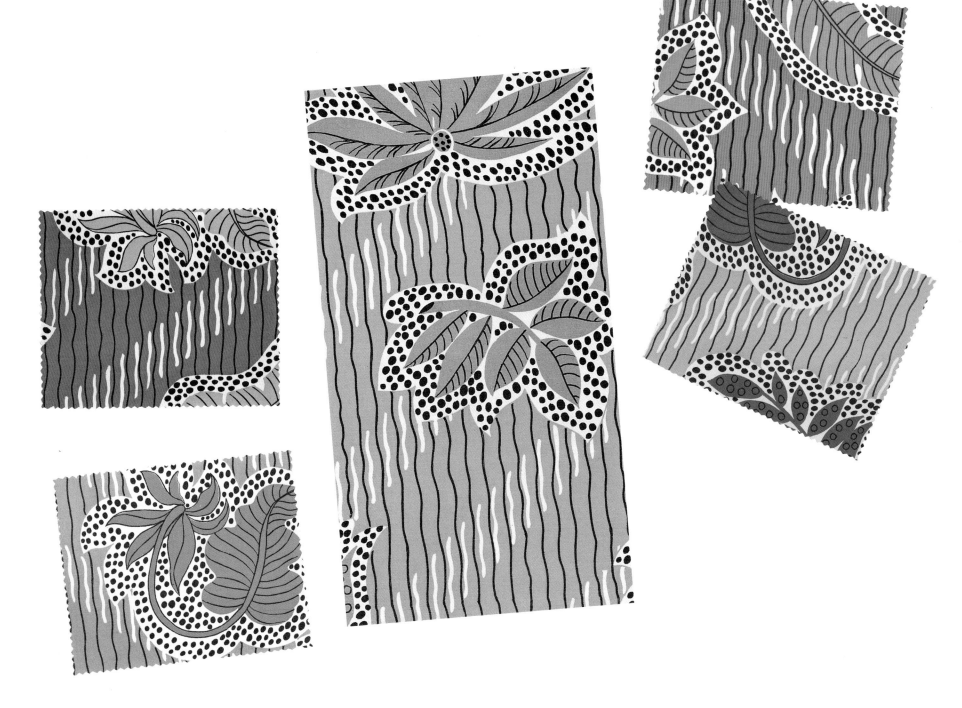

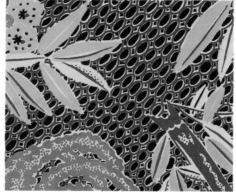

38

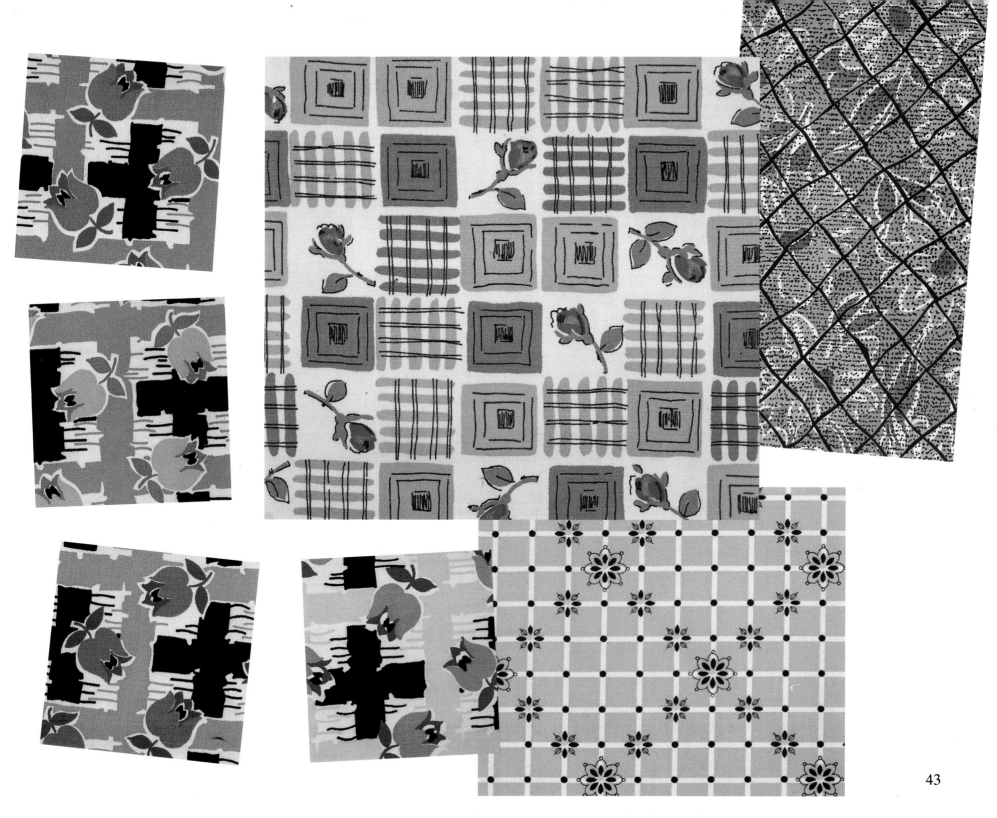

Geometric

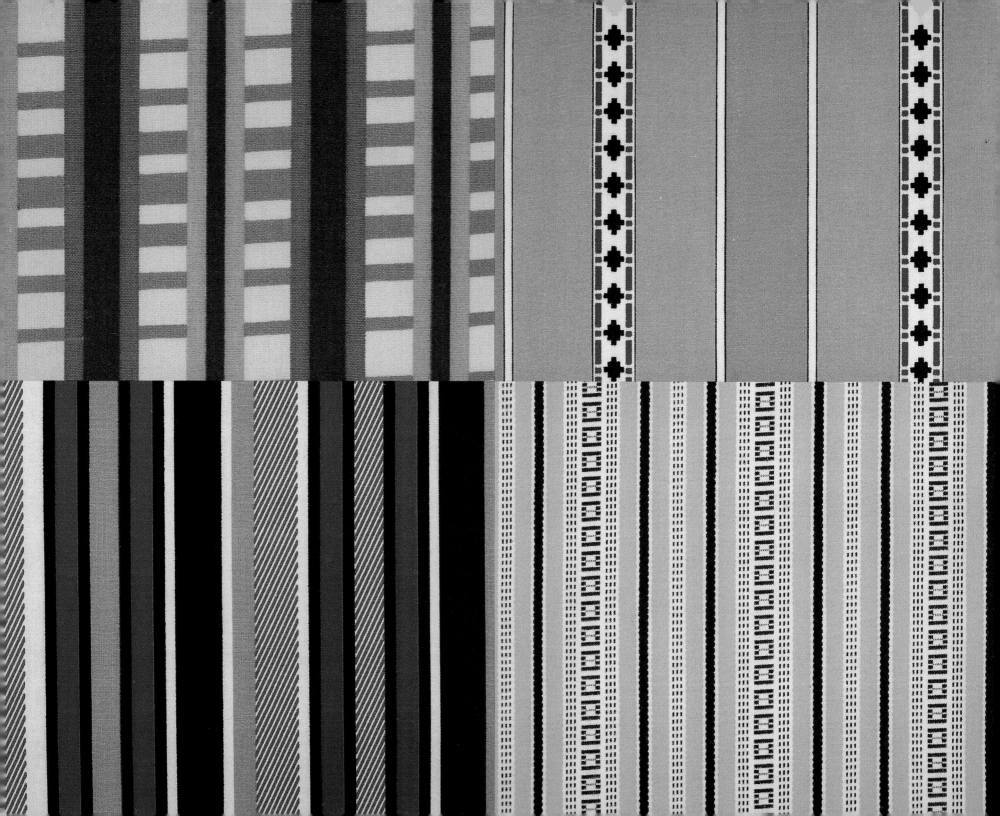

50

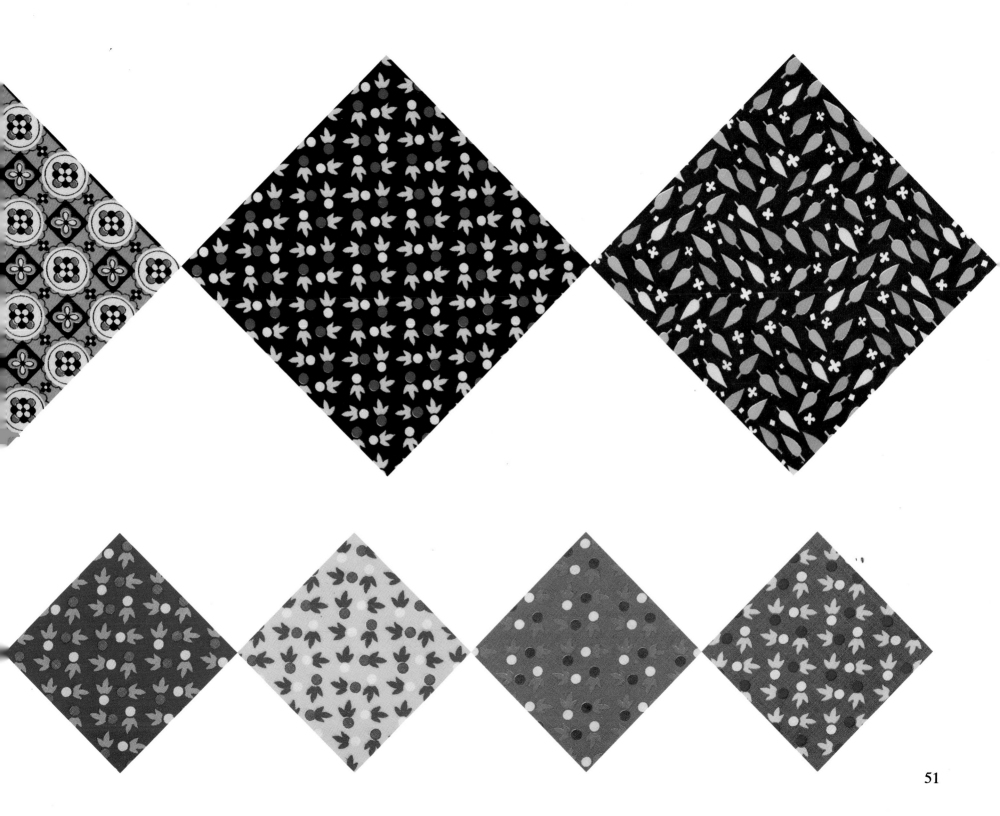

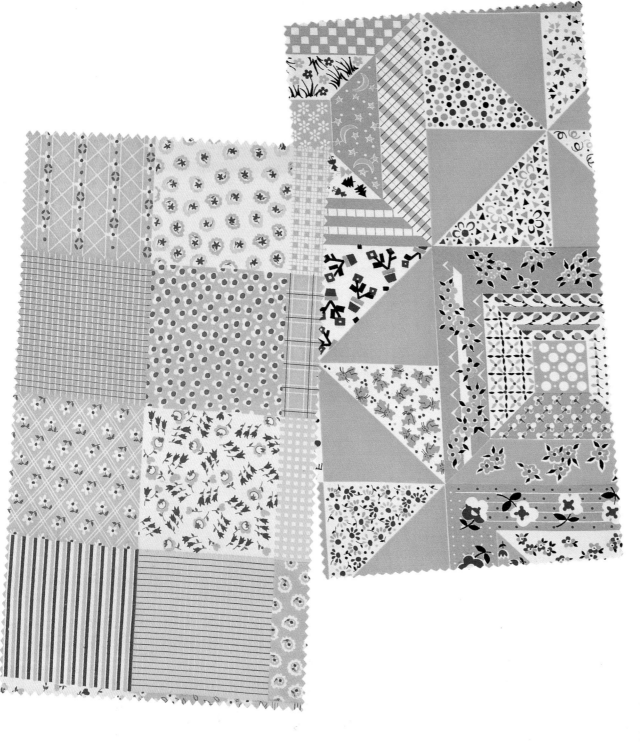

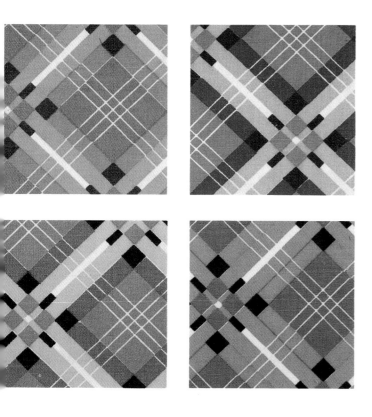

55

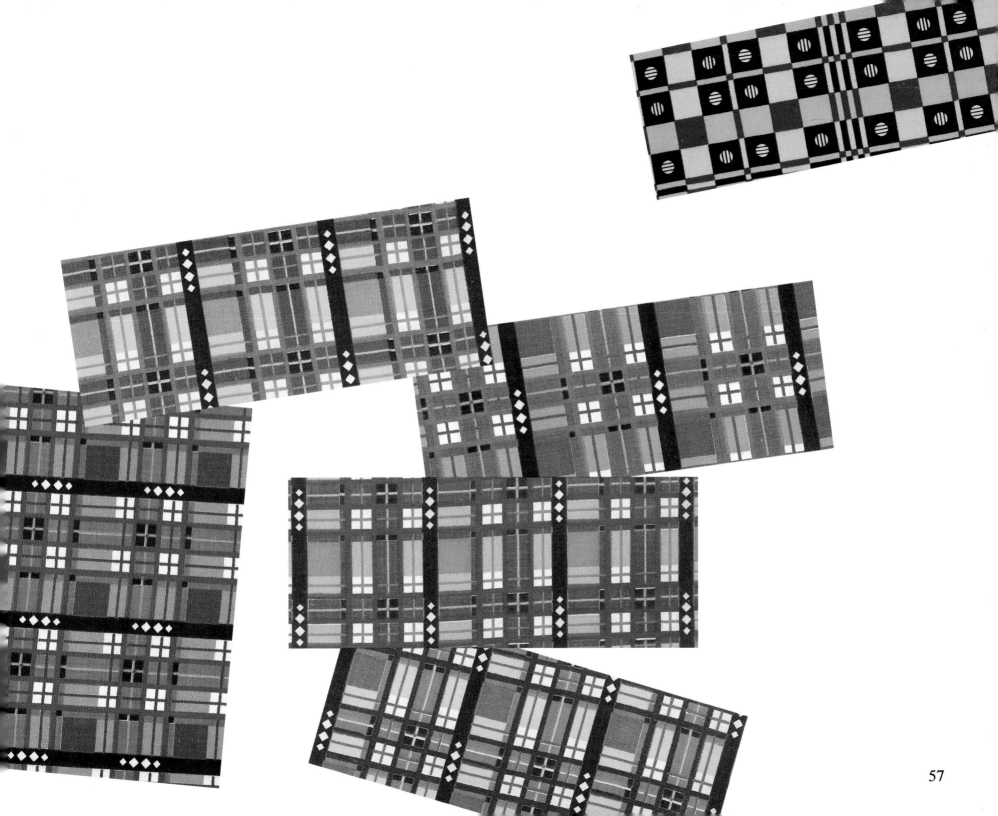

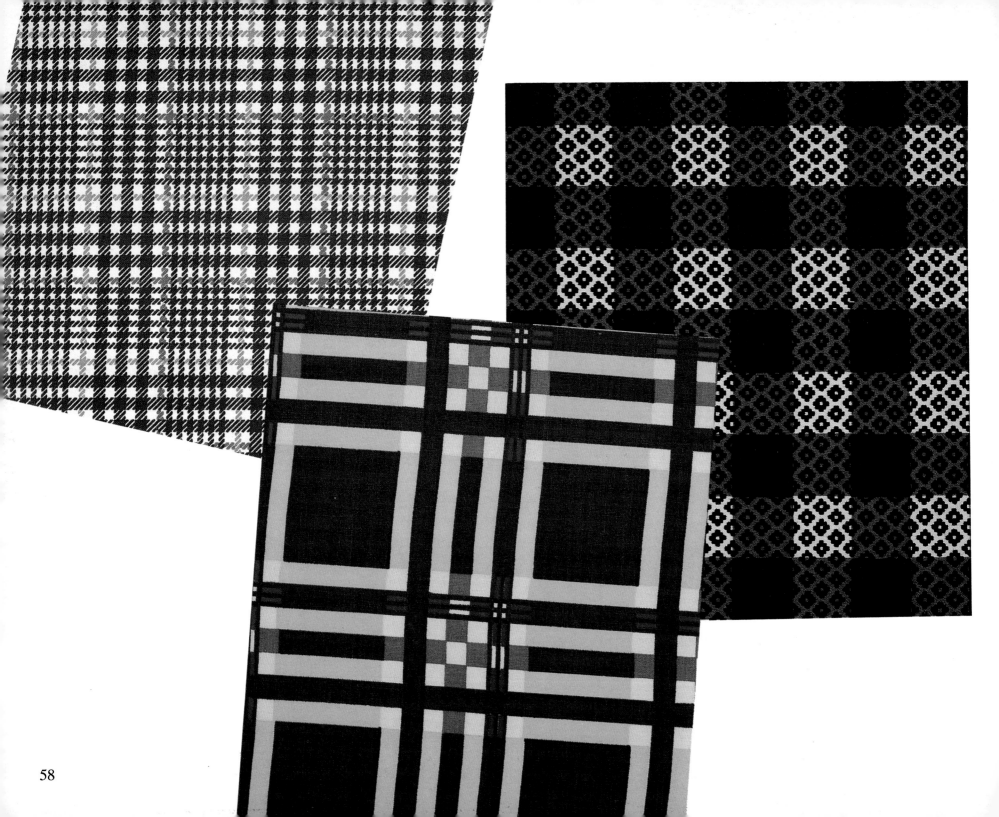

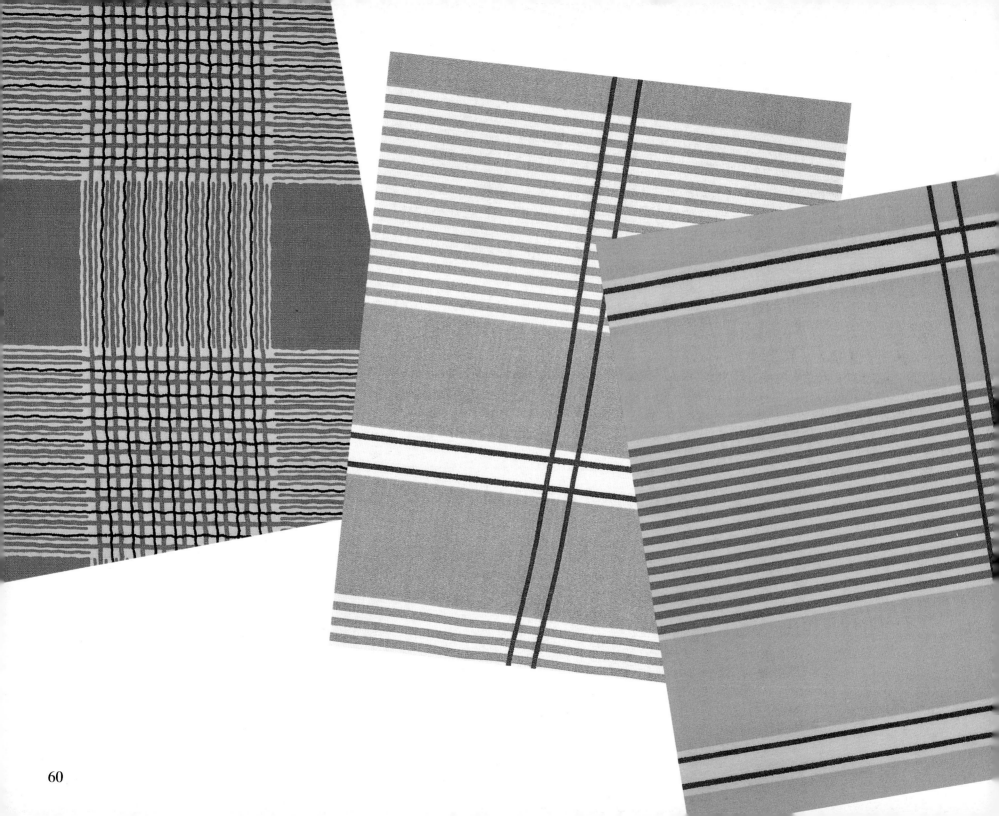

61

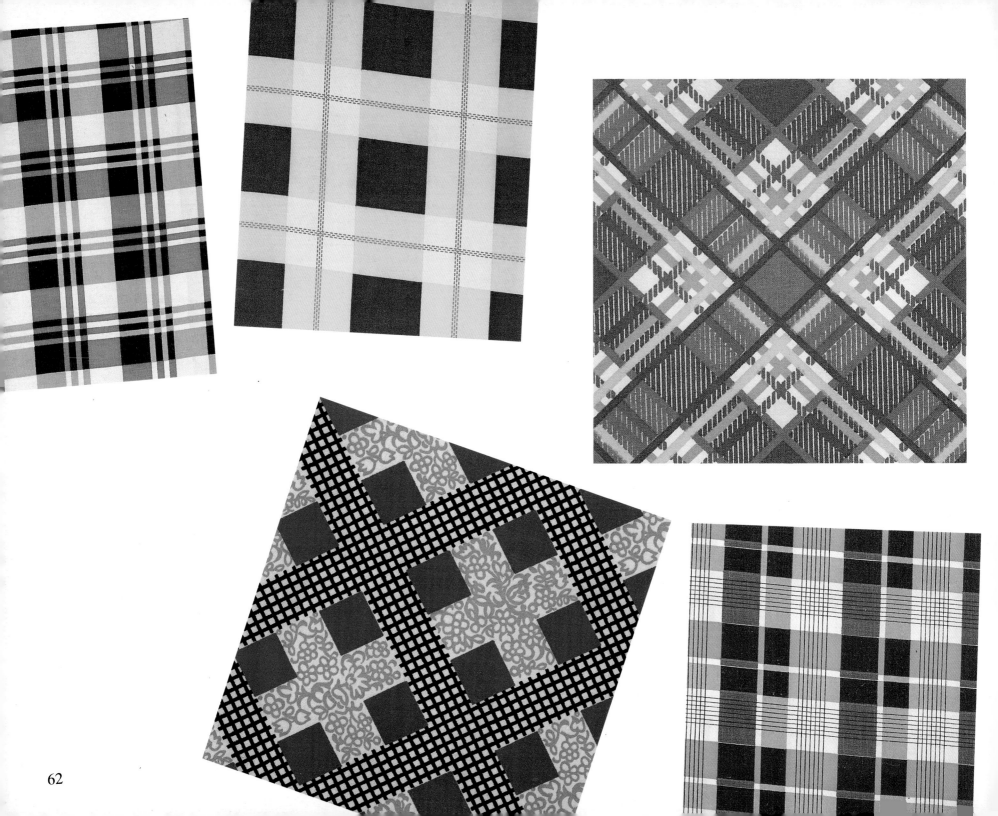

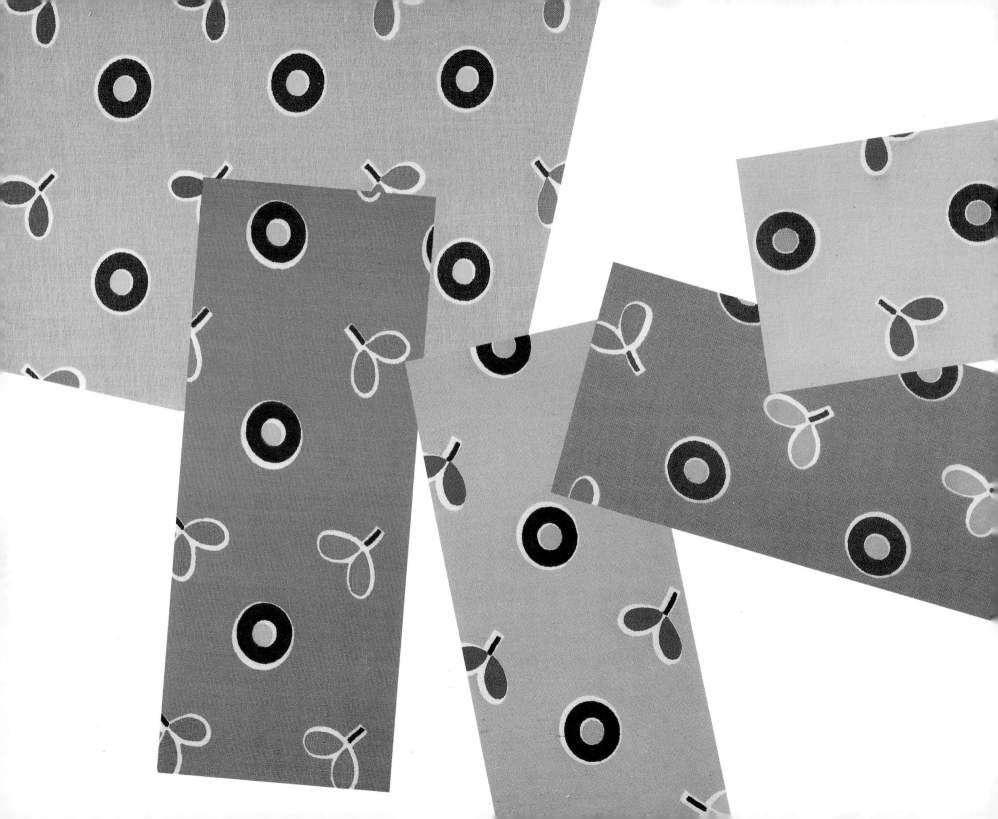

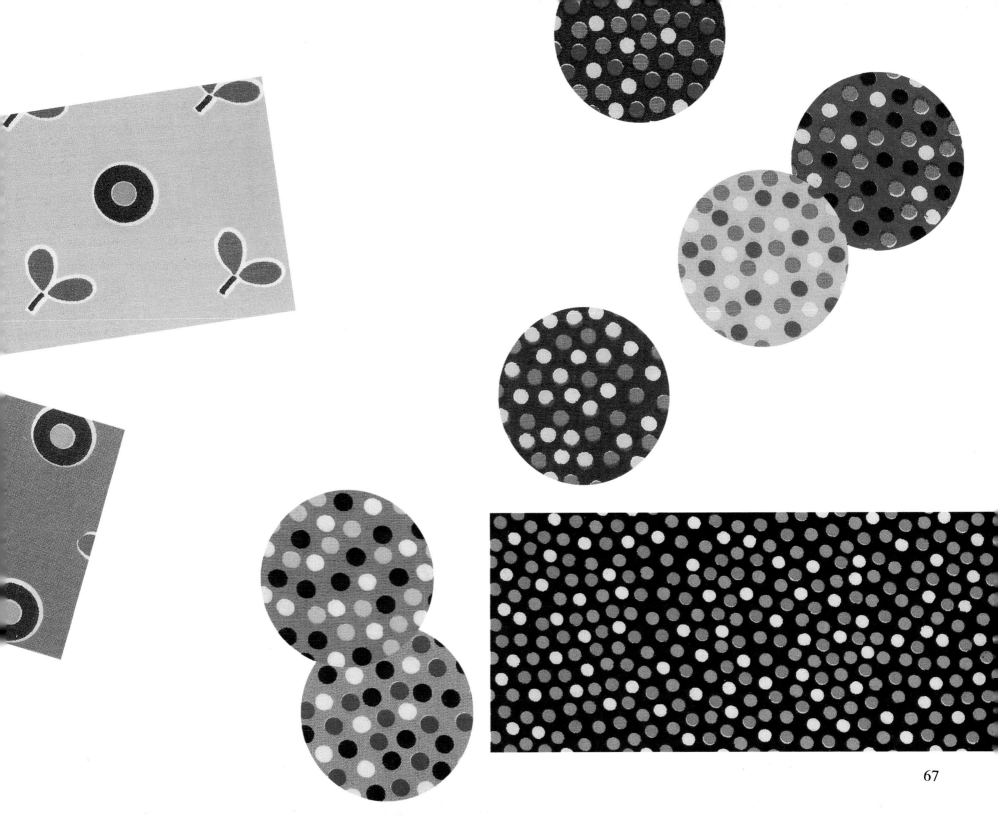

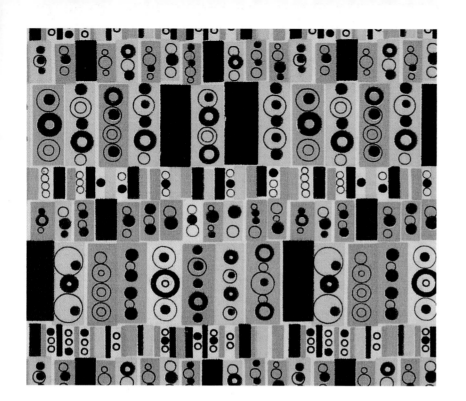

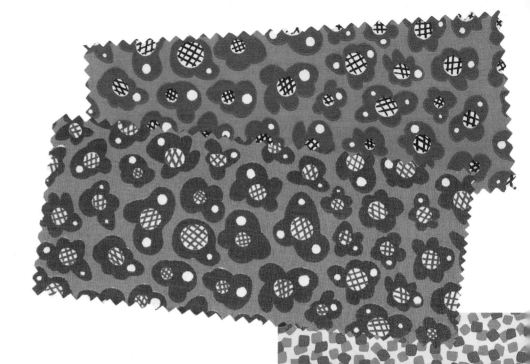

69

Novelty

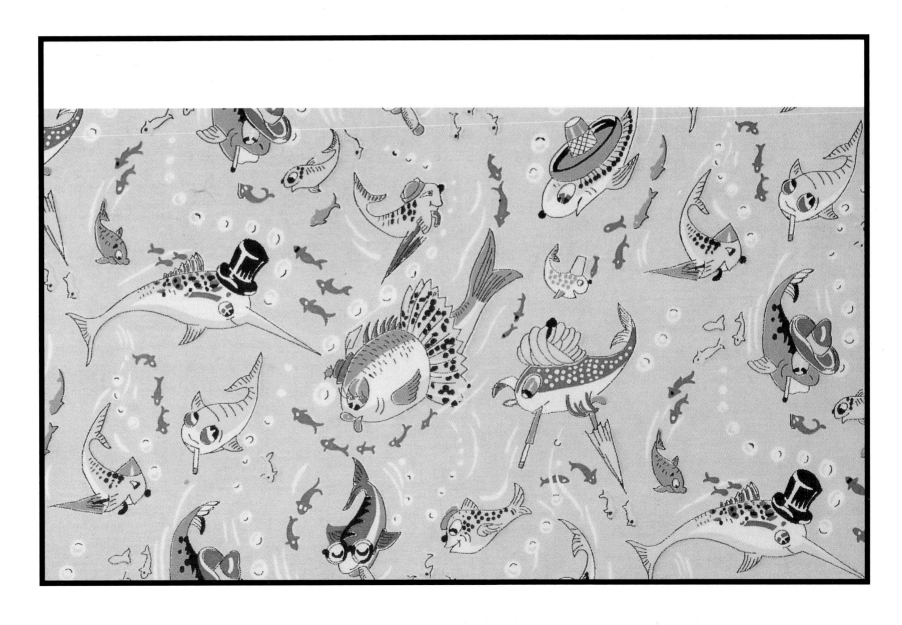

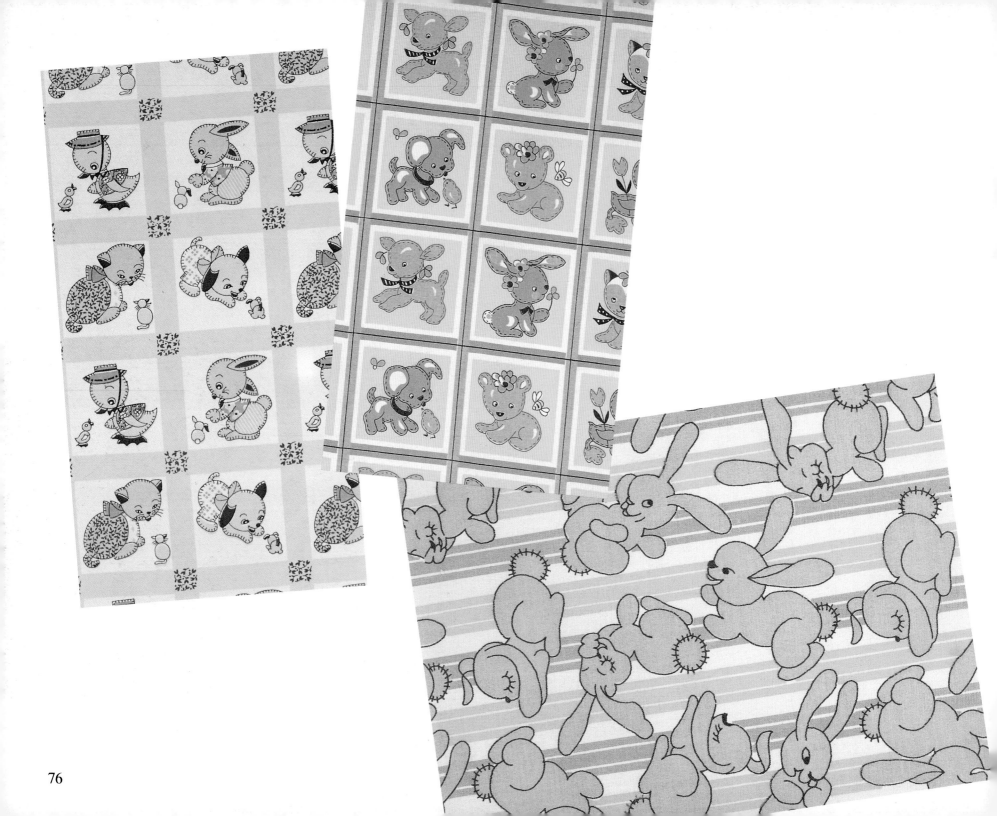

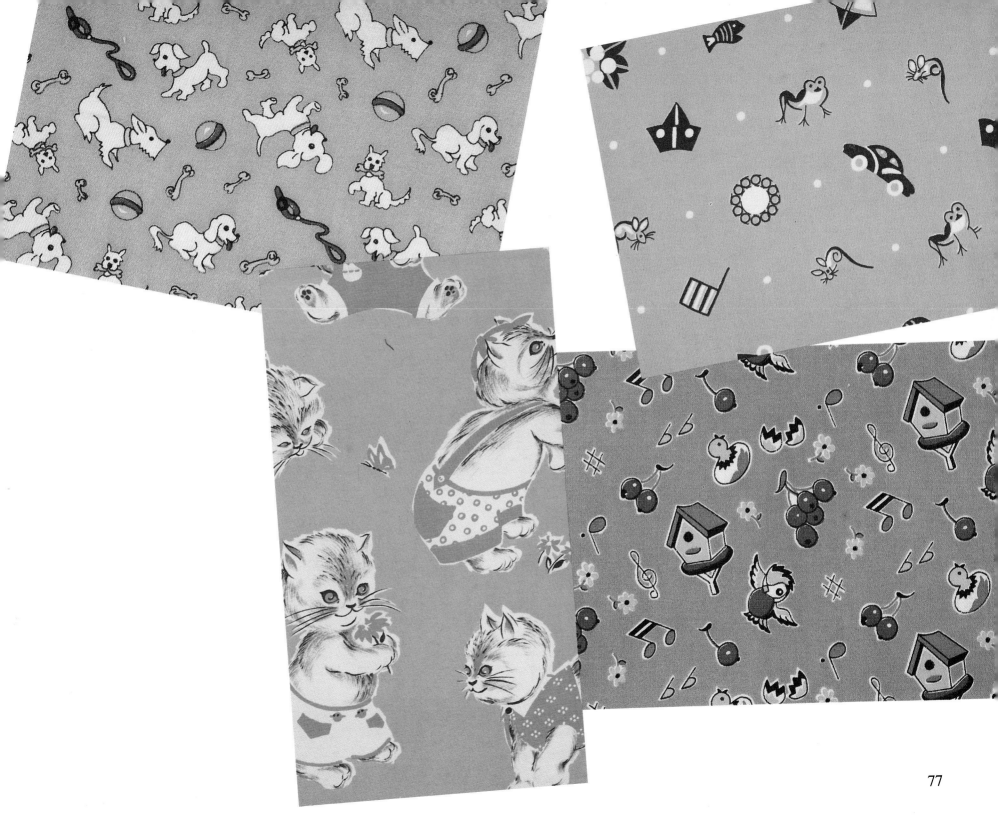

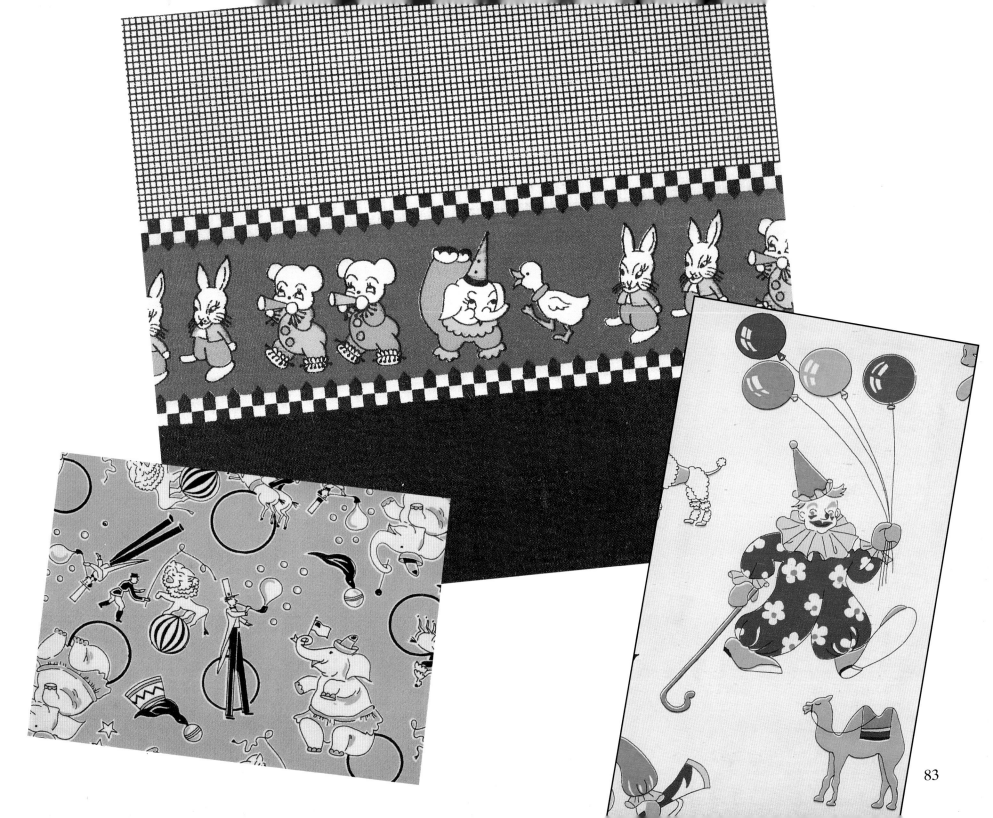

83

DEPERDUSSIN
1911

HENRY FARMAN
1914

WRIGHT BROTHERS
1903

BLERIOT MONOPLANE
1911

SANTOS DUMONT
1906

HENRY FARMAN
1914

WRIGHT BROTHERS
1903

MG TF

SIATA

JAGUAR

JAGUAR

ALFA ROMEO

FERRARI

MERCEDES BENZ

TRIUMPH

1910

1910

1904

MG TF

SIATA

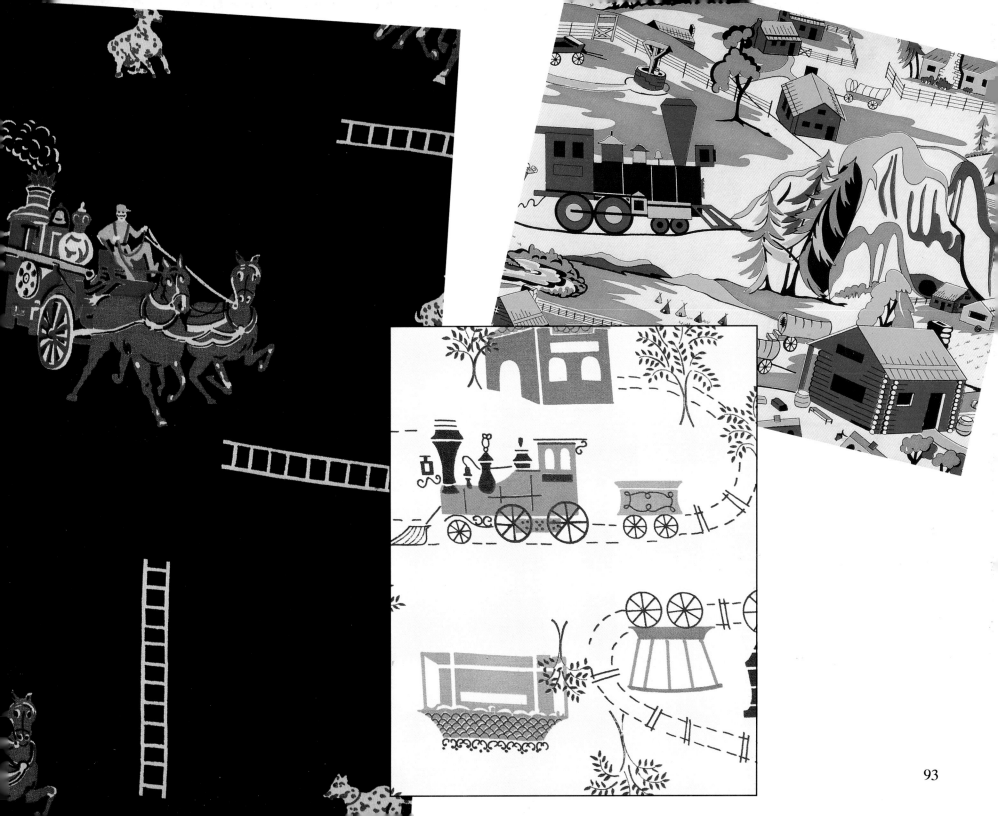

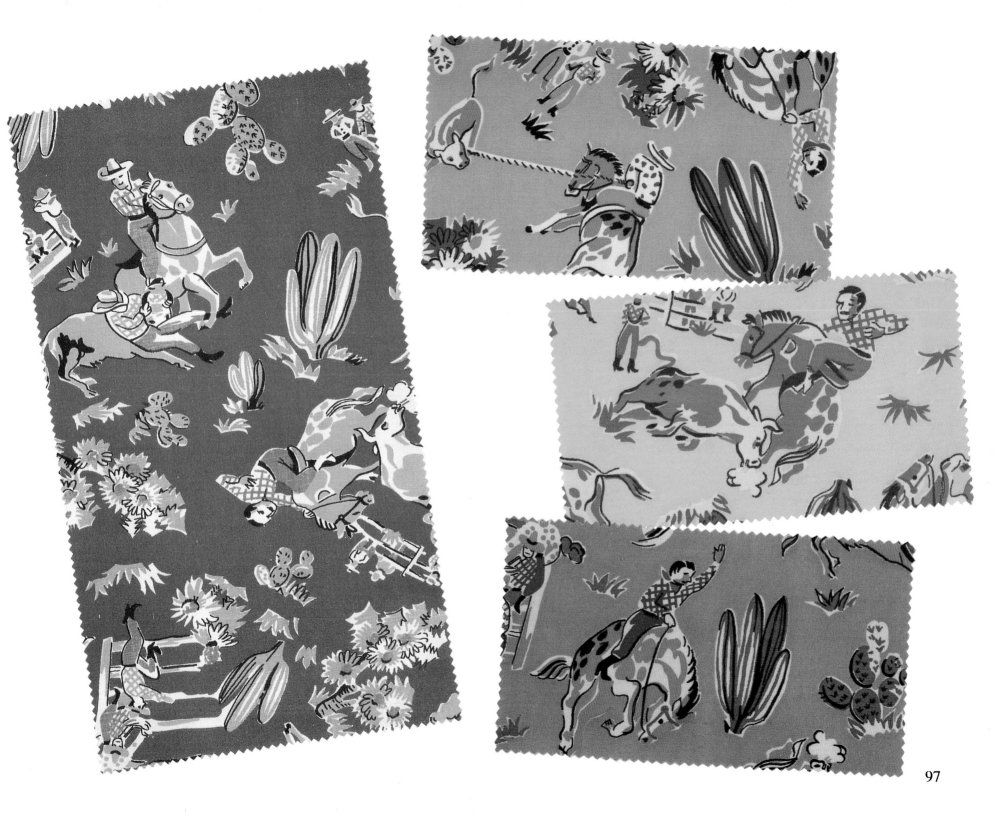

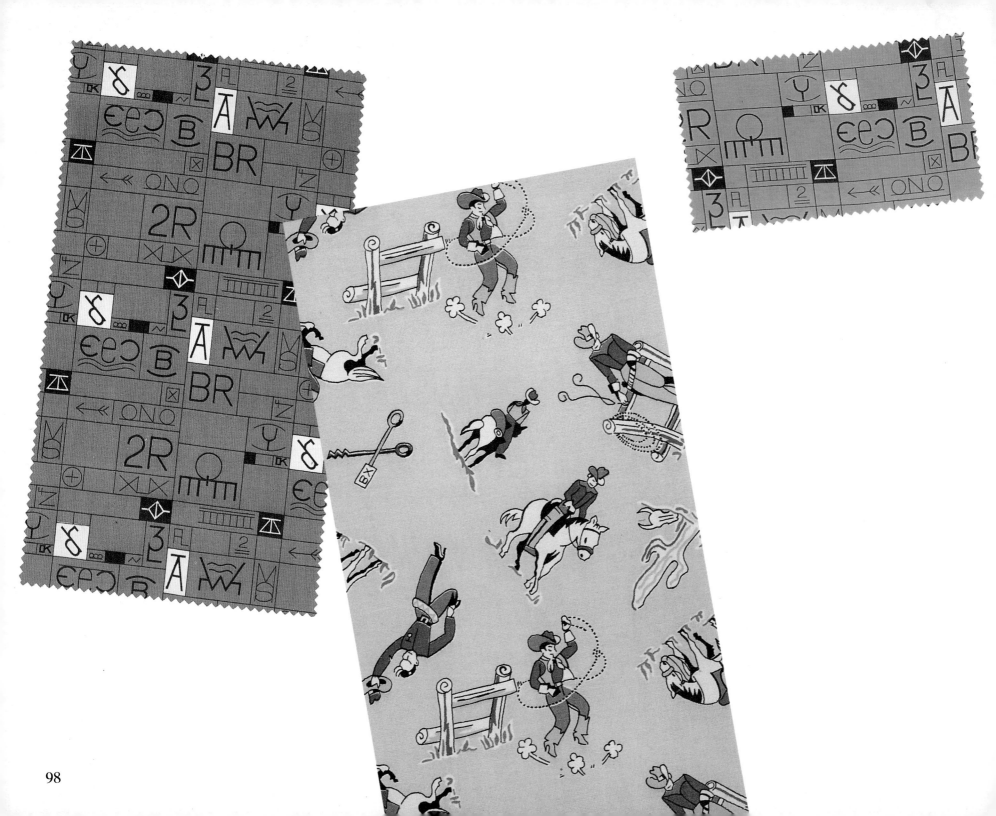

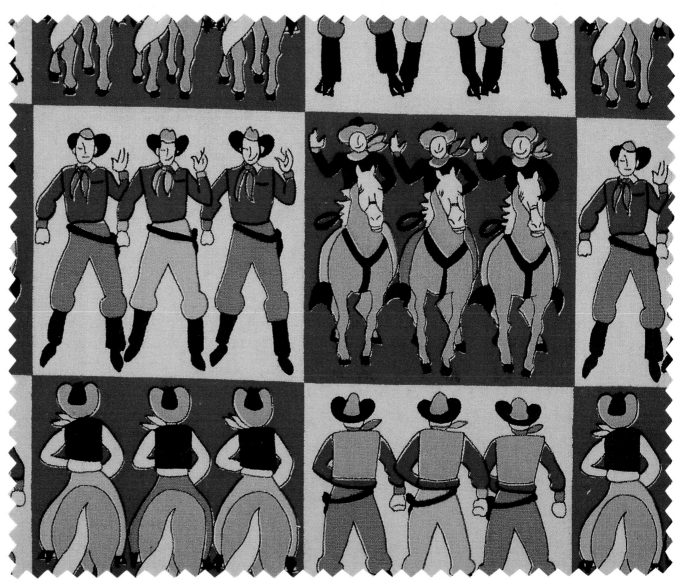

99

100

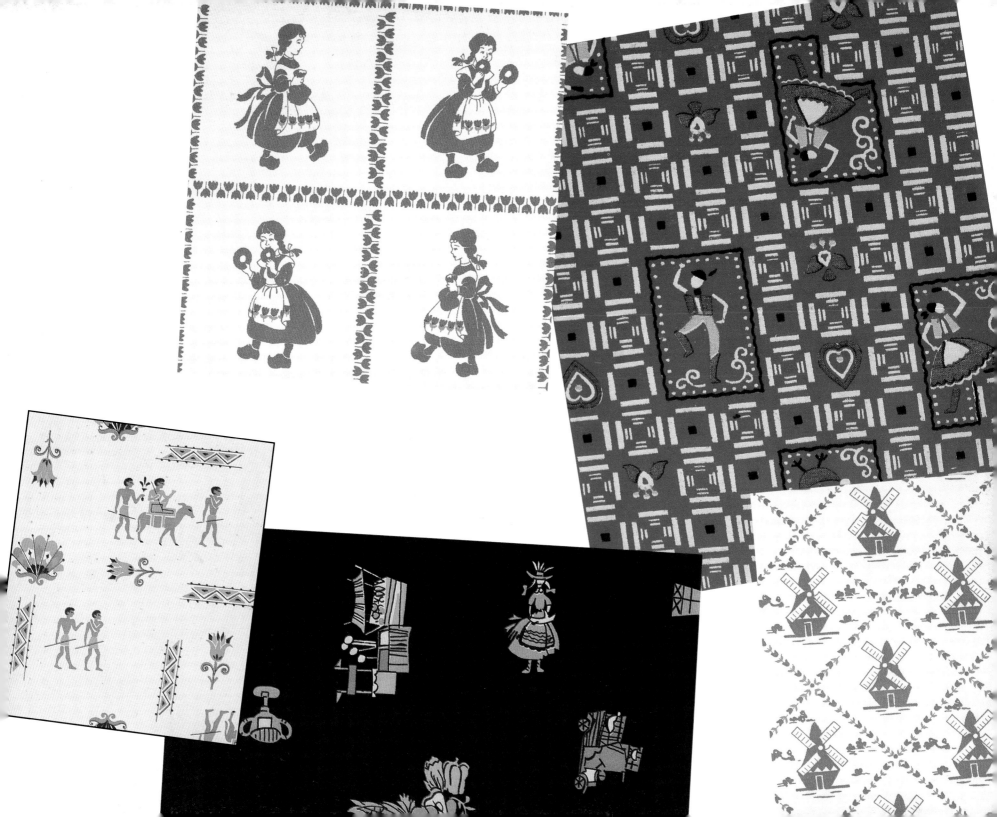